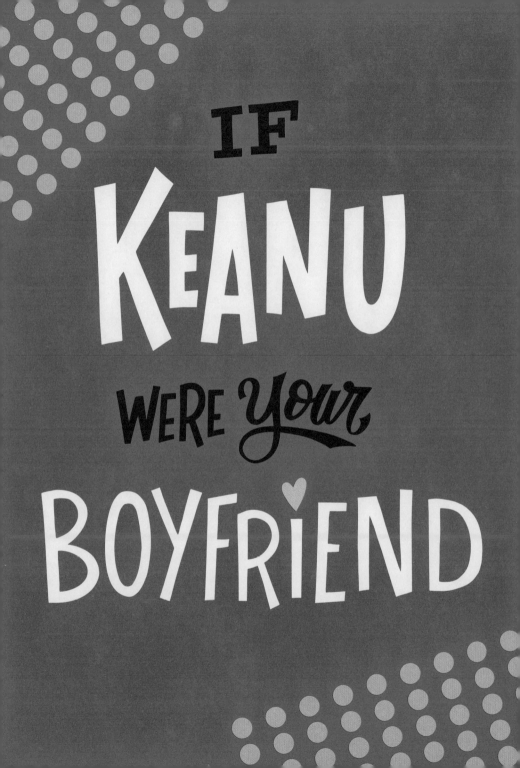

IF

KEANU WERE YOUR BOYFRIEND

THE MAN, THE Myth, THE WHOA!

By Marisa Polansky

LB

Little, Brown and Company
New York Boston

DEAR READER,

The man, the myth, the *whoa*. Keanu Reeves is one of the twenty-first century's most well-known and well-loved actors. And yet, what do we *really* know about Keanu?

When we consider his *excellent* career, well-reported good deeds, and decades of interviews brimming with quirky gems, all evidence suggests that Keanu is kindhearted, humble, thoughtful, and determined. In short, Keanu is the perfect boyfriend.

Before we go further, I must confess, Keanu Reeves is not my boyfriend, and he will probably never be, either. Well, at least not in this red-pill reality. And so, what follows is a dreamlike narrative (with no relation to the real Keanu whatsoever), featuring sixteen quotes taken from interviews with the unicorn-of-a-man himself.

Reader, this is your last chance. After this, there is no turning back. Take the red pill and the love story ends before it begins. Take the blue pill and dive into a world where anything is possible, even your relationship with Keanu Reeves.

With love,

Marisa Polansky

CELEBRITIES— THEY'RE JUST LIKE US.

Who doesn't love a normal boyfriend with the totally *normal* honor of being named the Sexiest Man Alive? Despite being one of the most famous (and miraculously unchanged) faces since his 1986 film debut in *Youngblood*, Keanu insists that he's lived a fairly ordinary life. And you know he's as low-key as he claims, since he's worn virtually the same outfit for years (jeans, T-shirt, and blazer often matched with a pair of beloved, taped-up boots). And while he's a notoriously massive motorcycle fan, he owns just two bikes. Not only does your everyman ride the New York City subway with the regular folk, but he's also not above casually parking himself on a bench for a snack. He's said, "I can move around the world pretty freely. No one freaks out." That's great because it means he probably won't mind popping into Walgreens for that two-for-one bodywash deal, so you can smell like him even when he's far away on the set of his next blockbuster.

WE'D FOLLOW KEANU ANYWHERE.

A guy as kind, humble, and polite as Keanu could come from only one place: Canada. However, Keanu Charles Reeves's journey started on the other side of the world, on September 2, 1964, in Beirut, Lebanon. Born to a British mother and an American father of Chinese-Hawaiian, British, and Portuguese descent, Keanu moved around with his family quite a bit before settling in Toronto, where he grew up playing ice hockey and managed to get expelled from high school. (Can you be expelled for being *too* perfect?) While his name means "cool breeze over the mountains" in Hawaiian, your global guy has a special way of heating up every room he enters.

WE'RE STILL IN LOVE, TOO!

Look, no one wants their boyfriend to claim he's "in love" with someone or something else, but you'll happily play second air guitar to Keanu's beloved career. While he's just "sweetheart" to you, don't forget he's also America's sweetheart. Keanu's decades-long career has produced over fifty of your all-time favorite movies. He has made us ROTF playing a caricature of himself in *Always Be My Maybe*, audibly cry as a dog-loving assassin in *John Wick*, and question our entire existence as a...uh, computer-programmer-turned-warrior in *The Matrix*. Just imagine Keanu being as committed to you as he is to his career and quoting (himself?!) from *Always Be My Maybe*: "Baby. I've missed you. I've missed you so much. I missed your heart. I missed your light. I missed your soul. I missed your spirit. I missed your eyes."

"WITH AGE COMES EXPERIENCE, OR WITH EXPERIENCE COMES AGE, ONE OF THE TWO."

DON'T CALL IT A COMEBACK.

Pop quiz, hotshot. You're dating a man who gets hotter and more interesting with every passing year. What do you do? What do you do?! Though he's solidly middle-aged and has been working in the film industry for decades, he's being hailed as the comeback kid. In the past five years, he's filmed six features, and the *Reevolution* shows no signs of stopping with the highly anticipated third *Bill & Ted* film in 2020, the franchise that solidified Keanu's place in the pop-culture canon and in our hearts. Just like John Wick, we're thinking he's back and we're hoping he never ever leaves.

LOVE IS A BATTLEFIELD.

You would be willing to don a hard hat, protective goggles, and a full hazmat suit if it meant Keanu Reeves would fall dangerously in love with you. Though the truth is, it's a little hard to know when he's fallen for someone. Keanu's personal life isn't often in the tabloids, and there are precious few photos of Keanu with confirmed girlfriends. Rumor has it he dated director Sofia Coppola and actor Parker Posey, but he's been reported to get down with the nonfamous folk, too—which bodes well for you. The truth is that Keanu's fairly tight-lipped about his life, and that's a good thing because you'll get to remain as anonymous as you've always been and he can be your own private Idaho.

HOME IS WHERE KEANU IS.

Who doesn't love a homebody? After all, why would you ever go *outside* your house if Keanu Reeves were *inside* your house? He's claimed to love nothing more than an ice-cold glass of chocolate milk and admitted to staying home alone on a particularly sad New Year's Eve. But life with Keanu won't be all Netflix and chill, which of course would be fine with you anyway. He's been quoted saying that on occasion he likes to pull out his records and DJ until four in the morning. If that means all-night dance parties with Keanu spinning songs from his band Dogstar, you'll be the first to say, "Party on!" and gladly adjust your morning routine and budget to include a double matcha latte and extra pairs of gold-infused eye masks.

STRONGER TOGETHER.

Keanu's life has included its fair share of tragedy. A tumultuous childhood had him moving between countries, forcing him to grow up fast. After coming to Hollywood, he suffered heartbreaks from the loss of friends and loved ones, including his close friend and *My Own Private Idaho* costar, River Phoenix. But through it all, he's remained resilient, vulnerable, and present. He says, "After loss, life requires an act of reclaiming. You have to reject being overwhelmed. Life has to go on....Life is precious." And life certainly will be precious when you two are side by side supporting each other.

KEANU, THE GREATEST THING SINCE SLICED BREAD.

It makes sense that Keanu's preferred food would be a favorite of the masses, since he's undoubtedly a man of the people. While his peers may have champagne wishes, his dreams are less caviar and more smoked meat. Your man is easy to please. His favorite sandwich is simple: "A hot pastrami sandwich, with Russian and mustard. On rye. With a kosher dill pickle. Sliced in quarters. With some potato chips. And a Coca-Cola on crushed ice." Okay, a touch particular, but still easily achievable. However, that's not the type of sandwich he was holding in the iconic 2010 "Sad Keanu" park bench photo, which is perhaps the reason it looks like an outtake from the end of *Sweet November*. Luckily, Keanu has said him being sad all the time is a misconception. He's a self-professed "happy-go-lucky guy." Well, of course he is! He has you and he has carbs.

DID YOU HEAR HIM SAY *WE*?!

Which iconic Keanu character uttered the words "The only true wisdom exists in knowing you know nothing"? Oh, never mind, that was Socrates (pronounced *So-crates*). But just like the famed toga-wearing philosopher, Keanu is a seeker of truth. (And would look excellent in a toga, too.) He's meditated with monks in the Himalayas, studied various schools of philosophy, and even played the Buddha in a movie. Dating a man with this level of enlightenment would make it blissfully impossible to fight over small things, like who left an empty milk carton in the fridge. If it ever did come to that, though, he'd probably gently say, "I believe that everyone has to search for and find his or her own answer." So, years from now, the two of you will find yourselves arm in arm in the twilight of your lives, searching for answers 'til the very end—ashes to ashes, stardust to stardust.

LOVE DON'T COST A THING.

In his multiple-decade-long career, Keanu's films have grossed over $4.9 billion in ticket sales. While Hollywood is known for being a volatile industry, there's no need to fret about Keanu's financial fate. Your man's ready to ride out the Hollywood wave Bodhi style with his other revenue streams. He's produced documentaries, directed films, and co-founded a production company. He turned his hog hobby into a career with his own motorcycle shop that builds and sells custom motorcycles. And he's even the author of *Ode to Happiness*, proving there's enough Keanu to go around. With all these diversified assets, you and your Renaissance man will never have to worry about your future kids' college funds.

SOME LIKE IT TOUGH.

It's hard to imagine that every day wouldn't be a walk in the clouds with Keanu, but when tough days inevitably come up, your boyfriend will be prepared to power through. Keanu is famous for performing his own stunts. He broke three ribs training for *John Wick: Chapter 3*, where he said he performed 90 percent of the action, studied for months in various martial arts, and became proficient in tactical gun training. On the set of *Speed*, the director warned him against the treacherous jump from a moving car to a speeding bus, but Keanu wouldn't be deterred. He rehearsed in secret, and on shooting day, he successfully made the leap. No matter how broken or bruised Keanu gets on set, he'll be lucky to have you there to nurse him back to health so he's at 100 percent and ready to say, "Vaya con Dios, brah."

YOU *CAN* JUDGE A BOOK BY ITS COVER.

Oh sweet, humble bibliophile Keanu. Yes, reading is *definitely* a hobby, and you'd even grab a copy of *The Lord of the Rings* (one of your man's favorites) if it meant curling up next to him in a book nook. Though the truth is that you don't need to escape into a fantasy land, because you've already got your happily ever after. Keanu is often mistaken for being an airhead like "Ted" Theodore Logan, but nearly everyone who knows him proclaims he's quite the opposite. He's been known to geek out on Proust and spontaneously recite Shakespeare sonnets from memory. Why yes, dear Keanu, you can compare us to a summer's day.

TO THINE OWN SELF BE TRUE.

Many people spend their days at work sending passive-aggressive e-mails, kissing up to bosses, and generally doing whatever is necessary to get by. There was a time many, many moons ago (known as the 1980s) when a young Keanu could be seen hawking Coca-Cola or Kellogg's Corn Flakes, but those days are long gone. Mature Keanu is a man of integrity. When Keanu was offered a huge payday to reprise his role in a sequel to *Speed*, your principled man turned it down to perform *Hamlet* at a regional theater company in Winnipeg, Canada. Years later he said, "Money is the last thing I think about," which frees him up to think about the way your hair glints in the light.

THE WAY TO KEANU'S HEART IS THROUGH HIS STOMACH.

Sharpen those knives and sign up for that cooking class that's been on your to-do list forever! Now is your time to shine. If you're making a column of "things Keanu does do" and "things Keanu doesn't do," you can now add exactly one thing to the right-hand side. On the left side are things like gives tons of money to charity, looks phenomenal in a suit, and is the "respectful king" of the internet—a moniker he received for posing with female fans without touching them. However, as his significant other, you'll be sure to get a full-impact hug when you offer to go shopping at the farmer's market to get ingredients for his favorite fall meal: Caesar salad with anchovies, a baguette, tomato soup with some sharp cheddar cheese, and a New York strip steak on the bone with some mashed potatoes and creamed spinach.

NO, KEANU, YOU ARE!

Fans at E3, the Electronic Entertainment Expo, lost their collective minds during Keanu's *Cyberpunk 2077* presentation when a fan screamed out "You're breathtaking!" Keanu's response was as magical as they come—he pointed right at the fan and hollered back "You're breathtaking!" But Keanu didn't stop there. He opened his arms wide and repeated those sparkling words to the entire audience.

Keanu is known as the nicest guy in Hollywood, and it feels as if everyone has a personal story about the actor with a heart of gold. Actor Octavia Spencer was on her way to an audition when her car broke down. No one stopped to help her. That is, until your knight in a shining motorcycle helmet saw her. He's been seen giving up his subway seat for other passengers, and he even entertained a van ride full of fellow stranded airplane passengers on an over-one-hundred-mile trip to the Burbank airport. He also reportedly took a pay cut on *The Devil's Advocate* to secure funding for Al Pacino. Keanu is Hollywood's champion, proving nice guys don't finish last.

LOVE NEVER DIES.

Perhaps your boyfriend's sole flaw—he won't live forever. But don't tell the internet....We can't have it breaking during the dawn of the *Keanusance*. In fact, Keanu's visage appears so suspiciously unchanged over the last thirty years that there's an entire website dedicated to proving Keanu's immortality. The site features historical portraits, some a millennium old, that bear his beatific face as proof. Sadly, Keanu debunked the theory himself. (But don't rule out the potential involvement of Rufus's phone booth time machine.) Even still, it's hard to believe a mere mortal could have responded to a question by late-night talk show host Stephen Colbert with this much profound tenderness. Colbert: "What do you think happens when we die, Keanu Reeves?" Reeves: "I know that the ones who love us will miss us."

CONTRIBUTOR BIOS

Marisa Polansky

MARISA POLANSKY

is a writer and cofounder of Speech Tank, a speechwriting company for all occasions. She lives in Brooklyn, New York.

VERONICA CHEN

is a tattoo artist and illustrator based in New York City. She doodles on skin, paper, and whatever else she can get her hands on. When she is not working, she enjoys traveling and embarking on one of her many DIY projects.

Veronica Chen

DIRTY BANDITS

Graham Burns

(aka Annica Lydenberg) is an art director, lettering artist, illustrator, and mural painter working with agencies and brands to create more authentic products, campaigns, and spaces. Work done by Dirty Bandits is fueled by Annica's deep appreciation for type, her interest in storytelling, and dedication to brands and individuals working for social good. Annica lives in Brooklyn, New York.

MARY KATE MCDEVITT

has created hand lettering and illustrations for clients including Target, Chronicle Books, Smucker's, and Macy's. She is also the author and illustrator of *Hand-Lettering Ledger*, *Illustration Workshop*, and *Every Day Is Epic*. Mary Kate lives in Philadelphia, Pennsylvania, with her cat, Peppy Mew Mew, and her old dog, Fritz.

Fred DiMeglio

JAY ROEDER

Dr. Nicole Roeder

is a hand-lettering artist, illustrator, and author. Jay's client work includes National Geographic, Hilton, American Greetings, Subway, Ray-Ban, Nike, and Facebook. Jay is the author and illustrator of *100 Days of Lettering* and *Lettering Alphabets & Artwork*. He works in a studio out of his Minnesota home, alongside his pugs, who sit on his desk while he procrastinates.

SELECTED SOURCE NOTES

"I'm just a normal guy" and "You're always fighting for a career.": Davis, Johnny, "The Esquire Interview Keanu Reeves," *Esquire*, December 11, 2017, www.esquire.com/uk/culture/film/a13033/keanu-reeves-john-wick-2-interview/. • "I can move around the world pretty freely....": Fleming, Michael, "The Playboy Interview: Keanu Reeves," *Playboy*, April 2006, http://www.whoaisnotme.net/articles/2006_04xx_kea.htm. "This has been an amazing journey.": Associated Press, "Keanu Reeves Gets Star on Walk of Fame," TODAY.com, February 1, 2005, www.today.com/popculture/keanu-reeves-gets-star-walk-fame-wbna6892728. "I'm still in love with acting and the movies.": Marchese, David, "Keanu's Excellent Directing Adventure," *New York Times*, October 18, 2013, www.nytimes.com/2013/10/20/movies/keanu-reeves-was-actor-an-director-for-man-of-tai chi.html?searchResultPosition=1. • "Baby. I've missed you. I've missed you so much....": Nahnatchka Khan, dir. *Always Be My Maybe*. 2019; Los Gatos, CA: Netflix, released May 29, 2019, https://www.netflix.com/title/80202874. • "With age comes experience, or with experience comes age. One of the two.": "Keanu Reeves Admits He Struggles with Action Films Now He's 50." *Irish Examiner*, March 25, 2015, https://www.irishexaminer.com/breakingnews/entertainment/keanu-reeves-admits-he-struggle-with-action-films-now-hes-50-669063.html. • "It's fun to be hopelessly in love. It's dangerous, but it's fun.": Fischer, Paul, "Keanu Plays Doctor New Romantic Comedy," Film Monthly, November 30, 2003, http://www.filmmonthly.com/Profiles/Articles/KReevesSomethingsGotta/KReevesSomethingsGotta.htm "I don't get out much.": Keanu Reeves, interviewed by Ellen DeGeneres, *The Ellen Show*, May 17, 2016, https://www.youtube.com/watch?v=waY6FwOd9eM. • "...an ice-cold glass of chocolate milk...," "Life good when you have a good sandwich," "A hot pastrami sandwich...," "Is reading a hobby?" "I don't cook wish I did. But I don't," "Caesar salad...," "I'm not immortal (unfortunately).": "Keanu Reeves—HELLO Reddit, October 13, 2014, https://www.reddit.com/r/IAmA/comments/2j4ce1/keanu_reeves_hello/. "...staying home alone on...New Year's Eve...": Keanu Reeves, interviewed by Graham Norton, *The Graham Norton Show*, February 10, 2017, https://www.youtube.com/watch?v=bctDr8ePsdU. • "...he likes to pull of his records and DJ until four in the morning...": "Keanu Reeves' late DJ sessions," Bang Showbiz, April 1, 2019, https://www.msn.com/en-ph/entertainment/celebrity/keanu-reeves-late-dj-sessions/ar-BBVXvJ "Grief changes shape, but it never ends" and "After loss, life requires an act of reclaiming....": Rader Dotson, "'I Don't Want To Flee From Life,'" *Parade*, June 11, 2006, http://www.whoaisnotme.net/articles/2006_0611_ido.htm. • "happy-go-lucky guy.": Stern, Marlow, "Keanu Reeves on 'Man of Tai Chi,' 'Bill & Ted' & 'Point Break,'" Daily Beast, updated July 11, 2017, www.thedailybeast.com/keanu-reeves-man-of-tai-chi-bill-and-ted-and-point-break. • "We're all stardust, baby.": Wiese, Jason, "Is Keanu Reeves Immortal? A Very Serious Fan Theory Investigation," CinemaBlend, June 21, 2019, www.cinemablend.com/pop/2475383/is-keanu-reeves-immortal-a-very-serious-fan-theory-investigation. • believe that everyone has to search for and find his or her own answer.": Blair, Richard, "Keanu Reeves Interview," ed. Anakin McFly, trans. Makee, *Penthouse* (Germany), March 2002, http://www.whoaisnotme.net/articles/2002_03xx_kea.htm. • "I like a tough day.": "Keanu Reeves: Work Drives Me," *People* (South Africa), April 8, 2015, http://www.whoaisnotme.net/articles/2015_0408_kea2.htm. • "...performed percent of the action...": Burwick, Kevin, "How Much Stunt Work Does Keanu Reeves Really Do in the John Wick Movies?" Movieweb, May 13, 2019, movieweb.com/john-wick-3-keanu-reeves-stunt-work-video/ "...the director warned him against the treacherous jump...": Miller, Leon, "20 Crazy Details Behind the Making of *Speed*." ScreenRant, September 4, 2018, screenrant.com/speed-movie-behind-scenes-deta-making-trivia/. • "I try not to do anything I don't want to do.": Freeman, Hadley, "Keanu Reeves: 'Grief and Loss, Those Things Don't Ever Go Away,'" *Guardian*, May 18, 2019, www.theguardian.com/film/2019/may/18/keanu-reeves-grief-loss--bill-ted-john-wick-actor-tragedy. • "Money is the last thing I think about.": Ebersole, Leo, and Curt Wagner, "'Money Is the Last Thing I Think...'" *Chicago Tribune*, May 30, 2003, www.chicagotribune.com/news/ct-xpm-2003-05-30-0305310043-story.html. • "You're breathtaking," Yam, Kimberly, "Just Keanu Reeves Telling A Crowd 'You're All Breathtaking,'" Huffington Post, June 11, 2019, www.huffpost.com/entrykeanu-reeves-breathtaking-e3_n_5cfe898fe4b0aab91c09b3d0. Stephen Colbert and Keanu Reeves quotes: Donaghey, River, "Keanu Reeves Told Stephen Colbert What Happens When We Die," Vice, May 13, 2019, www.vice.com/en_us/article/3k3k3w/keanu-reeves-told-stephen-colbert-what-happens-when-we-die.

Illustrations on cover, endpapers, title page (page 1), and pages 4, 14, 24, and 34 by Jay Roeder; illustrations on pages 6, 12, 22, and 28 by Dirty Bandits; illustrations on pages 8, 18, 26, and 30 by Veronica Chen; illustrations on pages 10, 16, 20, and 32 by Mary Kate McDevitt

Little, Brown and Company
Hachette Book Group
1290 Avenue of the Americas, New York, NY 10104
Visit us at LBYR.com

First Edition: November 2019

Little, Brown and Company is a division of Hachette Book Group, Inc. The Little, Brown name and logo are trademarks of Hachette Book Group, Inc.

The publisher is not responsible for websites (or their content) that are not owned by the publisher.

Library of Congress Control Number: 2019948235

ISBNs: 978-0-316-46101-6 (hardcover), 978-0-316-46098-9 (ebook), 978-0-316-46100-9 (ebook), 978-0-316-46103-0 (ebook)

Printed in the United States of America

WOR

10 9 8 7 6 5 4 3 2 1